IMAGES
of America

ROUTE 66
IN SPRINGFIELD

Along the 1926–1930 alignment of Route 66 through Springfield, the Sweney Service Station operated on the corner of Second Street and Capitol Avenue, as shown in this photograph looking north from the intersection. At rear left the new armory can be seen, and the spire of Trinity Lutheran Church rises above the buildings behind Sweney's. The Illinois State Capitol is across Second Street to the left, out of view. (Courtesy of Sangamon Valley Collection, Lincoln Library.)

ON THE COVER: Taken on grand-opening day in September 1950, this image shows Cozy Dog Drive In on South Sixth Street with a line of eager customers. Ed Waldmire invented the "Cozy Dog" back in his military days in Texas, but first called it a "Crusty Cur." His wife, Ginny, later successfully convinced him to change the name to Cozy Dog because it is too good to eat just one single, lonely one. (Courtesy of Sue Waldmire.)

IMAGES
of America

ROUTE 66
IN SPRINGFIELD

Cheryl Eichar Jett

ARCADIA
PUBLISHING

Published by Arcadia Publishing
Charleston SC, Chicago IL, Portsmouth NH, San Francisco CA

Printed in the United States of America

Library of Congress Control Number: 2010925749

For all general information contact Arcadia Publishing at:
Telephone 843-853-2070
Fax 843-853-0044
E-mail sales@arcadiapublishing.com
For customer service and orders:
Toll-Free 1-888-313-2665

Visit us on the Internet at www.arcadiapublishing.com

To my parents, Charlotte and Gene, who in 1962 took me from Illinois to California and back on Route 66 in a pink-and-white Dodge Coronet.

CONTENTS

ACKNOWLEDGMENTS

Grateful thanks are due to Curtis Mann, Melinda Garvert, and Beth Shetter at the Sangamon Valley Collection, Lincoln Library; Joe Sonderman, fellow Arcadia Publishing author and Route 66 postcard collector; Tom Huber and Arlyn Booth at the Illinois State Library; Sue Waldmire at Cozy Dog Drive In; Bill Shea Sr. and Bill Shea Jr. at Shea's Gas Station Museum; and Jeff Berg at the Springfield Convention and Visitors Bureau. Without the outstanding Sangamon Valley Collection at the Lincoln Library and much previous research and preservation on the part of many historians and Route 66 enthusiasts, this book would not have been possible. To my editor Jeff Ruetsche and publisher John Pearson, I offer thanks for guidance, patience, and encouragement. To my friends and family, I give loving thanks for your unfailing support. And to Jim, thank you for the love in everything you do.

INTRODUCTION

The new federal highway Route 66 was designated through Springfield in 1926. Springfield's population was about 65,000, and its citizens were experiencing the new mobility that the automobile created. After World War I, automobile sales were brisk throughout the 1920s until the Great Depression slowed sales of everything. Automobile shows were held in large facilities such as armories and arsenals. Fords were popular, and by 1920 the Ford Motor Company had sold over 1 million cars. Farmers and rural residents badly needed paved roads to ensure they could travel into towns and cities to sell produce and take care of other business. City residents needed produce and goods brought in on a dependable basis and at a fair cost. In Illinois, particularly, adequate and reliable roads were needed because of the industries throughout the state. An efficient route connecting the capital city of Springfield with Chicago and St. Louis was vital.

On a national basis, the Federal Aid Post Road Act was passed in 1916, appropriating $75 million to be distributed within the following five years. Five roads in Illinois were to receive a share of this funding, including the road from Chicago to St. Louis, which included sections of Illinois Route 4. In 1926, the American Association of State Highway Officials (AASHO) agreed on a set of minimum standards for highway design across the country and on a numbering system, using even numbers to designate east-west highways and odd numbers to designate north-south highways. Previously existing roads in some areas of the country would be spliced together to begin the process of creating a contiguous national highway system.

During the time AASHO was creating the U.S. highway system, Cyrus Avery, a veteran member of various highway associations, rose to the forefront of the process. A resident of Tulsa, Oklahoma, he wanted to see his home state benefit from the new highway. Avery also saw the importance of linking Chicago with the western states. The even number 60 had been chosen for the route; however, as the highway appeared under Avery's advocacy to be arcing toward Chicago instead of heading straight east, the eastern states objected to the number 60 being used. Avery continued to advocate for the "great arc" of the new highway in a northeasterly direction toward Chicago. The number 66 was available, and AASHO agreed on it. The path of Route 66 was laid out through the eight states of Illinois, Missouri, Kansas, Oklahoma, Texas, New Mexico, Arizona, and California. Avery has been called the "Father of Route 66."

Illinois, with more industry than some of the other states and the need for a strong Chicago–St. Louis corridor, already had considerable road infrastructure in 1926. Generally following the old Pontiac Trail and also the path of the Chicago-Alton Railroad, Illinois Route 4 was the obvious choice for designation as the new Route 66. The state's head start on infrastructure gave it an advantage. Illinois Route 4 was simply designated as Route 66. In addition, the last glacier to cover Illinois had scraped the landscape quite clean of obstacles, giving highway crews flat terrain on which to work.

The progressive era of the Roaring Twenties provided plenty of opportunities for use of the new Chicago–Los Angeles route. Due to the popularity of the automobile, Americans were intrigued with their new mobility. The nation's first sports agent, Charles C. Pyle, conceived the idea of a coast-to-coast footrace from Los Angeles. The First Annual Transcontinental Footrace, also known as the "Bunion Derby," was planned and promoted, offering close to $50,000 in prize money. On March 4, 1928, there were 275 runners leaving Los Angeles. Support staff and vehicles, including a shoe repair shop and a mobile radio station, accompanied them the length of Route 66 to Chicago. Only 65 runners were left in the race when the group left Chicago to run the last 1,000 miles of the race. Madison Square Garden in New York City was the finish line. Part-Cherokee Oklahoman Andy Payne won the race when he reached Madison Square Garden more than 15 hours ahead of the nearest competitor. It had taken Payne over 573 hours and five pairs of shoes. Payne became such a hero in his native state that famous humorist Will Rogers was nearly displaced as "Oklahoma's favorite son." In 1932, motorists headed west for the Summer Olympic Games in Los Angeles. The next year, travelers motored in the opposite direction to reach the 1933 World's Fair in Chicago.

External forces such as World War II in the 1940s slowed construction and maintenance on Route 66 across the country due to material and manpower shortages; however, during other eras, Route 66 itself positively affected the economy by creating highway construction and maintenance jobs. Along the route, at junctions and in communities large and small, restaurants, motor courts, motels, service stations, automobile garages and dealers, and attractions of all kinds sprang up to serve the traveler. Generations of families earned their livings pumping gas, dishing up dinner, building tourist cabins, and selling souvenirs.

Route 66 carried those going somewhere and those going nowhere. The truckers, the business travelers, the families on vacation, the newly homeless, and the free spirits all mingled in the lunchrooms and at the gas pumps along the new route. Literature and the entertainment industry had a new topic to cover.

But motorists increasingly wanted to get where they were going faster, and driving through cities slowed them down. Although initially the route connected the hearts of the cities, a pattern evolved whereby alignments moved farther and farther away from the city centers. Businesses flourished along new alignments and withered on old ones. In the 1950s the interstate network was born, and the pattern repeated itself.

Springfield followed this same pattern. The early Route 66 took travelers through the heart of the city past the Illinois State Capitol and other state buildings and just a couple blocks away from the downtown retail district, the fine hotels, and the old Illinois State Capitol, which then served as the county courthouse. The 1930–1940 route funneled motorists away from the downtown, bringing them down Ninth Street past a mixture of industries, utilities, budding hospitality businesses, and Abraham Lincoln's home. As traffic increased, another outward move to what was called Bypass 66 created the 1940–1977 alignment. Of course, the ultimate route change was to the new interstate I-55. As each alignment moved east farther out of town, businesses mushroomed and then withered.

Route 66 officially ended in 1977, and the last of the highway signs came down in 1985. In the 1990s, people began to express interest in preservation of the architecture along the famous highway and to document the route itself. This movement continues to gather momentum, enabling Route 66 to live on and new generations to explore and enjoy it.

One

ROUTE 66 IN

SANGAMON COUNTY

The 1926–1930 first alignment of Route 66 came through Williamsville and Sherman to the north of Springfield and exited the capital city through the village of Jerome before moving south through Chatham, Auburn, and Thayer and on into Macoupin County. This route took the traveler south to Carlinville. But by 1930, the demand for a more direct path that would go through fewer towns caused highway officials to change the route so as not to slow down the motorist. In the northern part of Sangamon County, highway sections were replaced, but the route remained basically the same. However, in 1930, the route south from Springfield was altered to flow from South Sixth Street through Litchfield. This meant that Chatham, Auburn, and Thayer had only four years to enjoy Route 66 business. The 1930 route came to be known as City 66 and utilized Peoria Road, Ninth Street, and Sixth Street to create a more or less straight path through Springfield. A decade later, a new route around Springfield, Bypass 66, was created. Bypass 66 turned off Peoria Road at the north end of the city, curved southeast, and then ran directly south on Thirty-first Street, later renamed Everett Dirksen Parkway. On the south side of Springfield, Bypass 66 turned east on Linn Avenue, later renamed Adlai Stevenson Drive, before hooking up with City 66 on South Sixth Street. From there it moved south alongside Glenarm before crossing into Montgomery County.

By the early 1900s, both federal and state officials, not to mention farmers, rural residents, and other travelers, realized the need to pave roads and move beyond the conditions seen in these two photographs. In 1900 there were 200,000 cars produced in the United States. Yet out of the nearly 100,000 miles of gravel or macadam roads in the country, Illinois only had about 8 percent. The State of Illinois began serious efforts to improve road conditions in the early 1900s. In 1905, a commission to study the Illinois road system was established, and in 1910, state licensing of vehicles was required, with the fees to go toward road construction. The Tice Road Act, which approved state bonds for roadway improvements, was passed in 1913. (Both courtesy of Library of Congress.)

A contemporary photograph of the preserved highway rest area at Sherman probably does not look much different than a vintage picture would. Early rest areas did not have modern conveniences like restrooms, coffee vending machines, and wall-mounted highway maps like 21st-century motorists enjoy. An early Route 66 traveler would count himself lucky to find a picnic table under a shade tree. (Photograph by Cheryl Eichar Jett)

The Carpenter Park segment is an abandoned quarter-mile section of roadbed that has not been in use by automobile traffic since 1936. Located north of Springfield in Springfield Township, it is a two-lane, 16-foot-wide example of 1922 highway engineering. Like other sections of highway, this was an existing road redesignated as Route 66 in 1926. (Photograph by Cheryl Eichar Jett.)

Known today as the Auburn Brick Road, this 1.53-mile section was originally part of State Route 4. It is a well-preserved example of early highway construction and contains two original single-span concrete bridges that were constructed in 1920. Another section of this historic segment was constructed in 1921, consisting of 1,277 feet of 16-foot-wide Portland cement. (Photograph by Cheryl Eichar Jett.)

In 1930, Route 66 was directed down South Sixth Street out of town to the south. In this view, roadwork is being done to prepare the new section of highway that curved around Copp's Corner. The Copp family was busy building a half-dozen new businesses to serve travelers as they rounded the corner of the new Route 66. (Courtesy of Sangamon Valley Collection, Lincoln Library.)

This section of highway was part of the Lake Springfield alignment and is at the curve of what is now Southwind Drive and North Cotton Hill Road, north of Lake Springfield. The route followed Sixth Street south of Springfield. Another segment south of the lake is also visible and is marked "Old Carriage Way." Both of these portions of Route 66 were in use before Lake Springfield was constructed. (Photograph by Cheryl Eichar Jett.)

This view is of a two-lane highway bridge over railroad tracks near Glenarm around 1940. Most bridges along Route 66 were constructed of concrete. This one features concrete balusters, railings, and piers. Many early highways followed the approximate path of the railroads. (Courtesy of Sangamon Valley Collection, Lincoln Library.)

Two

THE 1926–1930 ALIGNMENT

The new Route 66 came southward through Sangamon County from Williamsville and Sherman along the east edge of Carpenter Park and wound around the north and west sides of the Illinois State Fairgrounds on Taintor Road. Down North Fifth Street, the highway passed lovely Lincoln Park, historic Oak Ridge Cemetery, and the stately Brinkerhoff House, home to the fledgling Springfield Junior College. At North Grand Avenue, Route 66 turned west three blocks before again heading south on Second Street. This route brought motorists past residential blocks before arriving in downtown Springfield. Early Route 66 rolled right by the Illinois State Arsenal, the magnificent Illinois State Capitol, the Illinois Supreme Court Building, and the Centennial Building. Several fine hotels just a block or two off the route offered first-class lodging for those who did not camp along the way. More residences lined the route south of the capitol. Another jog to the west followed South Grand Avenue to West Grand Avenue (later renamed MacArthur Boulevard), which took the traveler south into a curved section of road that became Wabash Avenue. At this point, one entered the village of Jerome. Springfield's earliest alignment of Route 66 was typical of the era, bringing travelers to and through the heart of the city.

The Illinois State Fair was first held in 1853 on a wooded site 1 mile west of the newly constructed Illinois State Capitol. The fair was then hosted in a dozen different cities during its first 40 years. Springfield became its permanent home in 1894 on a 156-acre site donated by Sangamon County and Springfield. The brick-and-stucco main gate was constructed in 1910 facing Sangamon Avenue and remains the official fairgrounds entrance. (Photograph by Cheryl Eichar Jett.)

Just inside the main gate is the 30-foot-tall *Rail Splitter* statue created by Springfield native John Rinnus, a department store display director. The young, clean-shaven Abraham Lincoln was made from fiberglass in 1967 and stands in front of the Illinois Building. The fiberglass was molded over a wire frame using two telephone poles for the legs. (Photograph by Cheryl Eichar Jett.)

The Illinois State Fairgrounds Exposition Building—the "Queen of the Fair"—is shown in a photograph from about 1899. This was the first new structure built, and its cornerstone was laid on July 4, 1894. The stately redbrick building was constructed with iron framing and segmented, arched windows. An elevator with a 4,000-pound capacity provides access to the second level. (Courtesy of Sangamon Valley Collection, Lincoln Library.)

The Coliseum Building at the Illinois State Fairgrounds was constructed in 1901 as a large enclosed amphitheater with a show ring for horses. This photograph shows the oval-shaped, three-level structure around 1934. The first level was built of brick with limestone trim, which formed an open gallery of arched openings. These have since been enclosed with glazed brick. (Courtesy of Sangamon Valley Collection, Lincoln Library.)

This early fire station at the fairgrounds is shown in the 1890s. A later station, built in 1938 on the corner of Main and Central Avenues, has served since 1994 as the Illinois Fire Museum. It was opened to the public by the Office of the State Fire Marshal and houses an authentic 1857 horse-drawn hand pumper alongside a replica of the 1948 Ford used by the old fairgrounds fire department. (Courtesy of Sangamon Valley Collection, Lincoln Library.)

This view of the Oliver Farm Equipment tent was taken at the Illinois State Fair in 1929. The company was formed by a merger in April 1929 of four companies: Oliver Chilled Plow Works, the American Seeding Machine Company, Hart-Parr Tractor Company, and Nichols and Shepard Company. (Courtesy of Sangamon Valley Collection, Lincoln Library.)

A group of about three-dozen women pose in front of the Illinois State Fairgrounds Exposition Building in 1929. The fairgrounds devoted a building to women's activities beginning in 1899, when the original Women's Building was constructed. It burned to the ground just two years later, and a new Women's Building was completed in 1903. The State Fair School of Domestic Science for women was housed there. (Courtesy of Sangamon Valley Collection, Lincoln Library.)

Radio station WCBS had a popular booth in the Exposition Building in this *c.* 1934 photograph.
In the 1920s, Harold Dewing, a radio operator from Rhode Island, put a portable station on the
air with the call letters WCBS. However, on the East Coast, the demand for portables declined as
fixed-location radio stations became plentiful. Dewing headed for the Midwest, broadcasting from
several cities, including Springfield, and eventually set up a fixed station. (Courtesy of Sangamon
Valley Collection, Lincoln Library.)

The Illinois State Fairgrounds racetrack was built in the late 1800s and reconstructed in 1927. The 1-mile-long clay oval motor racetrack is known as the "Springfield Mile" and has hosted competitive auto racing since 1910. It held its first national championship race in 1934 under the American Automobile Association banner. The Springfield Mile is considered to be one of the fastest dirt tracks in the world. (Courtesy of Sangamon Valley Collection, Lincoln Library.)

After passing by the Illinois State Fairgrounds on the north and west sides, the 1926–1930 Route 66 crossed Sangamon Avenue and then passed Lincoln Park on North Fifth Street. Lincoln Park was acquired by the Pleasure Driveway and Park District in 1905 and consisted of 88 acres with access from all surrounding streets—Black Avenue, Fifth Street, Sangamon Avenue, and First Street. Oak Ridge Cemetery and the Illinois State Fairgrounds surround the park in addition to an established residential neighborhood. The northern part of the park has open, flat areas contrasted by rolling, wooded land to the west and south. The tall gaslights on the bridge were removed in 1920 due to damage from vandals. (Courtesy of Sangamon Valley Collection, Lincoln Library.)

Stone Bridge, Lincoln Park, Springfield, Ill.

Both the stone bridge and the handsome stone pavilion were designed by local architect George H. Helmle. J. S. Culver Stone Company did the stonework on both the bridge and the pavilion. In 1911, the bridge was constructed at a cost of $2,222. The original design and many features of the park remain the same. (Courtesy of Sangamon Valley Collection, Lincoln Library.)

A photograph taken in the 1910s shows the swimming hole in Lincoln Park—one can almost feel the cool water as the boys dive in. This picture appeared in the 1912 annual report of the board of trustees of the Pleasure Driveway and Park District. Later the swimming hole was closed, but eventually a swimming pool was constructed. (Courtesy of Sangamon Valley Collection, Lincoln Library.)

This octagonal wooden pavilion was built in the early days of Lincoln Park. Before the Pleasure Driveway and Park District acquired the site in 1905, it was known as Oak Ridge Park from the 1860s, when the Springfield Railway Company established a streetcar stop there. Oak Ridge Park and a section north of it, the "Carpenter Tract," eventually combined as "North Park" until it was renamed "Lincoln Park" in 1905. (Courtesy of Sangamon Valley Collection, Lincoln Library.)

LINCOLN MONUMENT SPRINGFIELD, ILL.
D-406

At 1441 Monument Avenue are Oak Ridge Cemetery and the tomb of Abraham Lincoln. This is the final resting place of Lincoln; his wife, Mary; and three of their four sons, Edward, William, and Thomas. The tomb was designed by sculptor Larkin Mead and is constructed of brick and granite. From the 72-foot square base, double sets of stairs lead to a terrace. Four bronze sculptures representing the Civil War services of infantry, artillery, cavalry, and navy surround the base of the obelisk. After Arlington National Cemetery, this is the second-most-visited cemetery in the United States. Five governors are also buried here: Ninian Edwards (1826–1830), William Lee D. Ewing (1834), William Henry Bissell (1857–1860), Shelby Moore Cullom (1877–1883), and John R. Tanner (1897–1901). The cemetery was founded in 1855. (Left, author's collection; below, courtesy of Sangamon Valley Collection, Lincoln Library.)

The Springfield Junior College was established in 1929 by the Ursuline Order nuns. Its doors opened on September 9, 1929, about two months before the stock market crashed. This Italianate mansion, originally the home of George M. Brinkerhoff, was used alternately as a space for classes, student housing, and administrative offices. Students called it "the Castle." Early classes at the school were job-training courses to retrain people after the stock market crash. (Courtesy of Sangamon Valley Collection, Lincoln Library.)

The Springfield Hospital and Training School began in the Dr. W. O. Langdon residence, a large Italianate home at the northwest corner of North Fifth Street and North Grand Avenue. The hospital was founded in April 1897 under the auspices of the Lutheran Church. Wings were added to the building in 1899 and 1904. In 1931, the bylaws of the institution were amended to allow the institution to become a general nondenominational hospital. The name was changed in 1941 to Memorial Hospital of Springfield. As the needs of the community grew, a $1 million fund-raising campaign began, and in 1943, a new 270-bed hospital opened at the corner of First and Miller Streets. (Courtesy of Sangamon Valley Collection, Lincoln Library.)

Motorists on early Route 66 and locals could get new tires at the Capitol 24 Tire Company at 208–210 North Sixth Street, just four blocks off the Second Street federal highway route. A full staff appears to be ready to mount the new Firestone gum-dipped balloon tires in this photograph from about 1929. (Courtesy of Sangamon Valley Collection, Lincoln Library.)

Another view of the Capitol 24 Tire Company and Firestone Warehouse shows a lineup of shiny 1920s automobiles ready to roll. Inside the store, racks of tires and inner tubes stood ready for installation. The company's sign suggested, "Invite us to your next blowout." (Courtesy of Sangamon Valley Collection, Lincoln Library.)

The Maid-Rite Sandwich Shop opened on the corner of Jefferson and Pasfield Streets in August 1924 and is still open for business at this same location. Two partners from Quincy opened the restaurant, but one sold out within a few weeks, leaving Clyde Holbrook to adopt the Maid-Rite franchise and run the operation. It is said to be one of the first drive-up restaurants in the country. (Photograph by Cheryl Eichar Jett.)

On the corner of Second and Monroe Streets stood the castle-like Illinois State Arsenal, constructed in 1901–1903. The huge facility was popular during the 1920s for holding automobile shows. The arsenal was destroyed by fire in 1934 at a loss of $900,000. Investigators found that the fire was apparently started intentionally by a 10-year-old boy, Cecil Kiper, who was reported to be reading from a book on "good citizenship" as the fire began to blaze. (Courtesy of Sangamon Valley Collection, Lincoln Library.)

In 1841, Rev. Francis Springer and eight Springfield citizens met to incorporate the first Lutheran church in Springfield. A triple-spired church was constructed in 1860 on Third Street and served the congregation for 29 years. The building in this photograph at Second and Monroe Streets was completed in 1889 and still serves the congregation. The architect was Charles Frederick May. (Courtesy of Sangamon Valley Collection, Lincoln Library.)

This bird's-eye view looks west and shows the Illinois State Capitol, the Centennial Building (far left), and the Illinois Supreme Court (front left). The Illinois State Capitol at Second Street and Capitol Avenue was completed in 1888 after 20 years of construction. The magnificent structure is 361 feet tall, which is 74 feet taller than the U.S. Capitol. (Courtesy of Sangamon Valley Collection, Lincoln Library.)

State workers and visitors could probably smell spring in the air and hear the sounds of automobile traffic if they were outside on this fine day in 1929. The photograph captured the scene at the intersection of Second Street and Capitol Avenue. The Illinois Supreme Court building is at upper left, and the Sweney Service Station can be seen at lower left. The Centennial Building is ahead on the right. The 10-foot, 6-inch bronze Lincoln statue at the right is in front of the Illinois

State Capitol. The statue was dedicated in 1918, the centennial of the first meeting of the Illinois General Assembly. The sculptor was Andrew O'Connor, whose commissions also included an equestrian statue of the Marquis de Lafayette in Baltimore and the Theodore Roosevelt memorial in Glen View, Chicago. (Courtesy of Sangamon Valley Collection, Lincoln Library.)

The Centennial Building was built just south of the capitol in 1918 to commemorate the 100th anniversary of the admission of Illinois to the Union as the 21st state. Two later additions in 1928 and 1966 changed the original rectangular shape of the building into a square. The structure is now known as the Michael J. Howlett Building, after Illinois auditor and secretary of state Michael J. Howlett. (Courtesy of Sangamon Valley Collection, Lincoln Library.)

Sweney's Gas and Oil Company was open for business on the northeast corner of Second Street and Capitol Avenue in these photographs from 1927. The photographer of the above picture is looking west toward the Illinois State Capitol, and the below picture is a view looking east from in front of the capitol building. (Courtesy of Sangamon Valley Collection, Lincoln Library.)

Looking down brick-paved Capitol Avenue to the west in 1946, the photographer who captured this shot had a great view of the Illinois State Capitol. At left, hidden by the trees, is the Illinois Supreme Court Building, which was completed in 1906. The Illinois State Library now stands where the trees were at right. (Author's collection.)

Hotel Abraham Lincoln, Springfield, Illinois

The Hotel Abraham Lincoln on the corner of Fifth Street and Capitol Avenue opened in 1925 to wide acclaim. It was designed by the Springfield architectural firm of Helmle and Helmle, and the luxuriously appointed hotel was "truly metropolitan," according to the *Illinois State Journal*. Unfortunately, it fell into disrepair, and in 1978, only 10 seconds and 625 pounds of dynamite were needed to bring the grand old hotel down. (Courtesy of Joe Sonderman.)

The Leland Hotel at Sixth Street and Capitol Avenue was built in 1866 at a cost of $350,000 for construction and furnishings. Horace S. Leland opened the fine new hotel on January 1, 1867. The Leland is said to be the home of the horseshoe sandwich, first made by a chef there in 1928. The chef is said to have taken the recipe to Wayne's Red Coach Inn where the popular dish is still served. (Courtesy of Joe Sonderman.)

In this view from the capitol, the arsenal and Trinity Lutheran Church can be seen across Monroe and Second Streets. The tall building in the rear of the photograph is the St. Nicholas Hotel, and the Myers Building is at far right. The original St. Nicholas was built in 1855 and was considered to be the largest and finest hotel in the city. Several building sections still stand and today serve as an apartment building. (Courtesy of Sangamon Valley Collection, Lincoln Library.)

If travelers needed something from the five-and-dime, they did not need to stray very far off Route 66. Three blocks away on Fifth Street was F. W. Woolworth Company, Myers Brothers, Altman's, and a host of other retail stores. At left, out of view in this picture, is the Old Statehouse square. (Courtesy of Joe Sonderman.)

Bell Miller grew up in a house on Second Street next door to the site where she would eventually have a luxury apartment building constructed. She hired architect George Helmle to design this three-story, yellow-brick building, which is known as the Bell Miller Apartments. The luxury apartments appealed to upper-middle-class tenants. Miller was a well-known Springfield florist for several decades. (Courtesy of Sangamon Valley Collection, Lincoln Library.)

This Watt Brothers Pharmacy was located on the northwest corner of South Grand Avenue and Pasfield Street. The photograph was taken around 1945. The four Watt Brothers—Val, John Jr., Dave, and Bob—all worked their way through the University of Illinois pharmacy school and returned to Springfield to open drugstores. Val worked in a Springfield drugstore as a youth and soon knew that was the career he wanted. He was the first of the brothers to attend pharmacy school, but the others soon followed. Later on, John Jr. opened the first Watt Brothers Pharmacy at Ninth Street and North Grand Avenue. Val was the owner of the location pictured on South Grand Avenue. Dave owned the store at Eleventh and Ash Streets, and Bob's pharmacy was located on South Fifth Street. (Courtesy of Sangamon Valley Collection, Lincoln Library.)

Motel SlumberLand was located at 1641 Wabash Avenue in Jerome. Mr. and Mrs. Louis G. Hagen were the operators. As with most motels of the time, the fact that the motel was air-conditioned was prominently displayed on the modernistic sign. This motel was typical of the type built in the 1940s and 1950s, a rectangular or L-shaped building with connected units. (Courtesy of Sangamon Valley Collection, Lincoln Library.)

The Octo Cabins and Trailer Camp were located on West Grand Avenue South, later renamed MacArthur Boulevard. Frank and Marie Williams opened the unique motor court in the early 1930s and kept it open for nearly 60 years. They also ran Williams Grocery Store at the same location for close to 40 years. The cabins were later dismantled and sold for playhouses and storage sheds to local residents. (Courtesy of Sangamon Valley Collection, Lincoln Library.)

Three

THE 1930–1940 ALIGNMENT

The 1930–1940 alignment of Route 66 brought motorists into Springfield on Peoria Road as in the first alignment, but along the east side of the Illinois State Fairgrounds. Heavy through traffic already needed to be routed away from the center of the city onto a more direct path. Ninth Street was chosen for a good portion of this route, which made sense, as Peoria Road angled onto the north end of Ninth Street. By this time, mom-and-pop motels, restaurants, and gas stations were becoming plentiful around the fairgrounds to serve Illinois State Fair visitors and other travelers. Much of Ninth Street had a decidedly industrial character, and along this route stood Sangamo Electric Company, Central Illinois Light and Power, J. S. Culver Stone Company, and the Central Illinois Ice and Cold Storage Plant. Tourist attractions, motels, restaurants, and gas stations were also sprinkled along the route, particularly around the Abraham Lincoln Home neighborhood. Well south of the downtown area, Route 66 jogged west three blocks to Sixth Street where it continued south out of town. Along South Sixth Street grew another large commercial area to serve the motorist, ranging from Copp's Corner, begun in the late 1920s, to the A. Lincoln Motel, built in the 1940s, to the drive-in theater and fast-food restaurants established in the 1950s and beyond. Lodging could also soon be found south of town around Lake Springfield after its construction in the 1930s. This route through Springfield became known as City 66.

In 1940, this was how Peoria Road looked north of Springfield near the waterworks. The Sangamon River is just to the north. Peoria Road was designated as Route 66 and carried traffic into Springfield from Sherman, Williamsville, and other points farther north. (Courtesy of Sangamon Valley Collection, Lincoln Library.)

Virtually hidden from Peoria Road below, the Mernin's Court sign, now overgrown with vegetation, is a disappearing remnant of a family lodging business. Behind the sign on this embankment is a house and a few cabins, which are in slightly better condition than the sign. Small tourist courts, like this one with a handful of cabins in a row, sprang up all along Route 66. (Photograph by Cheryl Eichar Jett.)

The Ann Rutledge Motel, located in a beautiful setting with many tall trees, was about 3 miles north of Springfield. Eleven modern units were carpeted and air-conditioned and featured televisions, thermostatic-controlled heat, and tub-and-shower combinations. There was a spacious playground, and the motel was open all year. (Courtesy of Joe Sonderman.)

The Springfield Motel at 4421 Peoria Road was located on Route 66 North, just north of Bypass 66. They advertised "cleanliness, comfort, quiet, modern, showers, air cooled, electrically heated, family units." The sign frame is still there. (Courtesy of Joe Sonderman.)

LOCATED IN THE LAND OF LINCOLN
On U. S. 66 near Junction of North By-Pass 66 at Springfield, Illinois
Noted for Cleanliness, Comfort, and Courtesy. We will be pleased to advise you
in regard to good restaurants, Lincoln Shrines, and other points of local interest.

Another postcard view of the Springfield Motel assured salesmen that they were "always welcomed." A playground for children, picnic tables, and barbecue grills had been added, and there were "good restaurants nearby." Springfield Motel was a member of the American Motel Association and also carried the American Automobile Association (AAA) logo. (Courtesy of Joe Sonderman.)

Little Chum's Lodge at 4333 Peoria Road was constructed in 1951. It was a brick, rectangular-shaped, one-story building with a gable-end roof. Little Chum's consisted of 14 units. The building remains, but is no longer used as a motel. (Courtesy of Joe Sonderman.)

AAA - PIONEER MOTEL - U.S. 66 AT NORTH BY-PASS - SPRINGFIELD, ILL.

The Pioneer Motel was built at 4321 Peoria Road in 1951. Its construction consisted of brick, permastone veneer, and a wood frame, with two gabled-roof buildings creating an L-shape. There were 12 units. As its name indicated, the Pioneer had a frontier theme, complete with a buggy, wagon wheel decor, and the name "Pioneer" emblazoned on an arrow-shaped sign. The motel was advertised as "AAA recommended." The Pioneer Motel is still standing and in use, but the wagon wheel decor is no longer there. A radio tower–style sign holds a "Pioneer Motel" sign. (Courtesy of Joe Sonderman.)

Poineer Motel AAA Recommended, Route 66 at North 66 By-Pass, Springfield, Illinois

The Haven Motel on Peoria Road offered singles, doubles, and family units. This lodging was built as separate cabins with gabled roofs and porch overhangs at a tree-lined location along Route 66. The Haven Motel no longer exists. (Courtesy Sangamon Valley Collection, Lincoln Library.)

Poland's Modern Court north of Springfield at 4201 Peoria Road carried the American Automobile Association (AAA) logo on their postcards and advertised that their units had steam heat. (Courtesy of Joe Sonderman.)

A later postcard from Poland's Motel showed their "ultra modern" expansion. Poland's Motel offered radio, television, air-conditioning, and electric heat. Children and pets were welcome, and restaurants were nearby. Just "10 minutes from the heart of Springfield," Poland's was a member of the Springfield Motel Association. (Courtesy of Joe Sonderman.)

These two postcard views of the Capitol Motel at 4129 Peoria Road proclaimed it to be the "North's finest." It offered television, radio, room-controlled electric heat, air-conditioning, and ceramic tile baths. Three kitchenettes were also available. The Capitol Motel was a member of the American Motel Association (AMA), the American Motel and Hotel Association (AMHA), and the Springfield Motel Association. In this arrangement, the office and operator's quarters were in front to the right. Three rectangular buildings in a row contained the motel units. (Both courtesy of Joe Sonderman.)

At the time this postcard was produced, the Northern Aire Motel at 2915–2917 Peoria Road consisted of 16 modern units with ceramic tile tub-and-shower combinations, wall-to-wall carpeting, Heywood-Wakefield furnishings, televisions, and telephones. "Your comfort is our greatest concern," read their slogan. The Northern Aire is still located near the Illinois State Fairgrounds and right across the street from the Lazy A Motel. (Courtesy of Joe Sonderman.)

The Lazy A Motel was built in 1948–1949 at 2840 Peoria Road on approximately 2 acres of land. The 13-unit, U-shaped building was constructed in Southwest Vernacular style with stuccoed concrete block walls and a flat roof. Typical Southwest Vernacular decorative elements, such as projecting wooden vigas, cast-iron railings, and decorative tiles, were part of the original design. Originally all but one of the motel units had its own closed garage, but over the years most of these have been converted to kitchens or bedrooms. The Lazy A still stands but has been converted into apartments. The landmark has been on the National Register of Historic Places since 1994. Note the western-style wood gateway with steer's head in the view below. (Both courtesy of Joe Sonderman.)

Mr. and Mrs. L. R. Ross owned and operated the Ross Motel at 2127 Peoria Road. The "first motel south" of the Illinois State Fairgrounds featured eight fully modern units with all new panel heat, air-conditioning, and Simmons Beautyrest mattresses. The Ross Motel was a frame, one-story, rectangular-shaped building with a gable-end roof consisting of eight units. The building is still there, converted into several apartments. (Courtesy of Joe Sonderman.)

Bill Shea's Texaco Station at 2001 Peoria Road is pictured during the World War II era. Shea bought out his partner, Maurice Dupuy, in 1946. Maurice's nickname was "Mud," which apparently everyone agreed was more suitable for a gas station proprietor than the French "Maurice." (Courtesy of Bill Shea Sr.)

Another view of Shea's Texaco Station on Peoria Road during the 1940s shows the "Victory USA" shrubbery next to the street. Shea, a World War II veteran, now spends his days in his Shea's Gas Station Museum a few doors north of the Texaco station. The old station still stands, but the addition of siding has changed its look. (Courtesy of Bill Shea Sr.)

By 1955, Shea's Texaco Station on Peoria Road sported a fresh coat of white paint, and the shrubbery no longer adorned the edge of the pavement. Shea operated the Texaco station from 1946 until 1955, when he moved up the street, where he opened and operated a Marathon Station until 1982. (Courtesy of Bill Shea Sr.)

A propellerless airplane, built by Oliver Topliff in the garage behind Benny's Tavern next to Shea's Texaco Station, stands in the driveway at 2001 Peoria Road in 1934. The plane was built without a propeller and instead used flaps, visible on the front edges of the wings, to fly the plane. It had a very modern look to it. This driveway next to the Texaco station is on the west side of Peoria Road, and the houses visible are on the east side of the street. (Courtesy of Bill Shea Sr.)

Murrel Hampton is standing by Topliff's plane in this 1934 shot. The neighborhood grocery market is visible behind the house. The Texaco station is at right, out of view, and Peoria Road is between the market and the house, shown on the opposite side of the road. (Courtesy of Bill Shea Sr.)

From left to right are Oliver Topliff (builder of the plane), Murrel Hampton, and George Andruskevith in this 1934 view of the propellerless plane. The plane's numbers are visible on the wing. It is said that the plane later disappeared, and its existence was denied. (Courtesy of Bill Shea Sr.)

At left is Texaco Station regular Joe Kleckatz with Bill Shea Sr. in a Texaco uniform holding young Bill Shea Jr. in 1950. Visitors can now go to Shea's Gas Station Museum and meet both Bill Sheas. They operate Shea's Gas Station Museum in the building at 2075 Peoria Road, which was formerly Shea's Marathon Station; they welcome visitors with tours and stories. (Courtesy of Bill Shea Sr.)

The Capitol City Motel is on the east side at the bend where Peoria Road flows into North Ninth Street. Located at 1620 North Ninth Street, this is a classic motel that was in business during the Route 66 era and is still in operation. Route 66 fans cannot miss the bright-yellow block sign. (Photograph by Cheryl Eichar Jett.)

Peoria Road runs diagonally northeast to southwest across Sangamon Avenue to Ninth Street. Just south of the bend in the route is this viaduct. On this residential block, the view is looking south on Ninth Street (City 66) toward the viaduct. This photograph was taken by James A. Woodruff who captured many street and building scenes around Springfield in the 1970s. (Courtesy of Sangamon Valley Collection, Lincoln Library.)

This view of the North Ninth Street viaduct is looking in the opposite direction to the north. The photograph was taken at the intersection with Converse Avenue in 1970. The Sangamo Electric Company was located just off the picture to the right at North Ninth Street and North Grand Avenue. (Courtesy of Sangamon Valley Collection, Lincoln Library.)

The intersection of North Ninth Street/City 66 and North Grand Avenue/Illinois 29 is captured in this 1969 shot. On the northeast corner is Sangamo Electric Company, which manufactured electric meters. The company was formed in 1899 with Jacob Bunn Jr., Henry Bunn, and Ludwig Gutmann as officers. In 1943, sales reached a new high of more than $11 million and there was a wartime peak of 3,080 employees. (Courtesy of Sangamon Valley Collection, Lincoln Library.)

Another view of the same intersection shows Sangamo Electric Company on the northeast corner, Sinclair Station on the southeast corner, Standard Station on the northwest corner, and the Watt Brothers Pharmacy sign at the southwest corner. This view was taken from the Land of Lincoln Bank parking lot in 1968. Now Walgreens has replaced Watt Brothers, and CVS Pharmacy has replaced the Sinclair Station. (Courtesy of Sangamon Valley Collection, Lincoln Library.)

Enos Park still has the charm of an older, historical park, as well it should. The park was acquired in 1905 and is one of the oldest neighborhood parks. Its 3.5 acres are bounded on three sides by Enterprise Street on the south, Seventh Street on the west, and Eighth Street on the east. Many of the historical homes around this park in the north-central part of the city are undergoing restoration. (Photograph by Cheryl Eichar Jett.)

Stevie's Latin Village, operated by Stephen Crifasi, was considered to be one of Springfield's premier supper clubs. Located at 620 North Ninth Street, it featured a full menu, comfortable club chairs, and plenty of decorative scrollwork on several levels. This photograph shows the interior as it looked in November 1954. (Courtesy of Sangamon Valley Collection, Lincoln Library.)

Tony Crifasi is shown in the kitchen of Stevie's Latin Village. Several Crifasi brothers and a sister were involved in the restaurant business in Springfield. The family was originally from Palermo, Sicily. (Courtesy of Sangamon Valley Collection, Lincoln Library.)

In the kitchen at Stevie's Latin Village are Rose Crifasi (left) and "Mimi" Licata. (Courtesy of Sangamon Valley Collection, Lincoln Library.)

The staff at Stevie's Latin Village poses for a picture in the kitchen. Later, although the kitchen had been said to be fireproof, much of the interior of the once-fine restaurant was destroyed by fire. (Courtesy of Sangamon Valley Collection, Lincoln Library.)

This neglected-looking view of the Stevie's Latin Village building, looking south on Ninth Street at Miller Street, shows what the *Springfield Sun* called "Tombstone Corner" in 1969. The restaurant closed in 1972. Since then, a number of other restaurants occupied the building until its purchase and demolition by Springfield Electric in 2009. The corner property now consists of one small frame house surrounded by a bare dirt lot. (Courtesy of Sangamon Valley Collection, Lincoln Library.)

A shot of Ninth Street looking north from Carpenter Street shows a variety of small businesses in this commercial area close to St. John's Hospital. Note the Derby gas station sign at far left and the Route 66 sign just under the speed limit sign at center right. (Courtesy of Sangamon Valley Collection, Lincoln Library.)

This view of St. John's Hospital is from Madison Street. Four sisters of the Hospital Sisters of the Third Order of St. Francis were dispatched from Germany to Springfield in 1875 with little money and less English to care for the sick and the poor. They began their mission in the old Jacob Loose residence on South Seventh Street, making it their home and base of operations as they traveled by horse and buggy to treat patients. (Courtesy of Sangamon Valley Collection, Lincoln Library.)

This photograph shows the old St. John's Hospital chapel in September 1967. In 1878, the cornerstone was laid for St. John's hospital. The St. John's Hospital School of Nursing was founded in 1886, making it the first Catholic hospital school of nursing in the United States. Now the St. John's Hospital complex occupies nine city blocks and is bounded by Madison, Ninth, Carpenter, and Sixth Streets. (Courtesy of Sangamon Valley Collection, Lincoln Library.)

The J. S. Culver Stone Company building is shown here as it looked in 1969. The castle-like structure was regarded as a landmark in the city. Col. James S. Culver was born in Ohio in 1852 and came to Illinois at a young age. After several years in the stone and marble business in Taylorville, he moved to Springfield in 1883 and established his stone contracting business. (Courtesy of Sangamon Valley Collection, Lincoln Library.)

Culver served as the builder of many important buildings in Springfield including the State Armory as well as the Memorial Temple to Illinois troops at the Vicksburg (Mississippi) Battlefield. A 1912 issue of the *Journal of the Illinois State Historical Society* stated, "He was a businessman of the highest type. Scrupulously honest, he was more than fair in his dealings with his associates." He died in 1911. (Courtesy of Sangamon Valley Collection, Lincoln Library.)

According to the motel's postcard, the Downtowner Motor Inn was located at 400 North Ninth Street "between Lincoln's home and Lincoln's Tomb." It offered television, hi-fi, a heated swimming pool, free parking, free reservation service, private meeting rooms, and ultra-modern accommodations "in the heart of downtown." (Courtesy of Sangamon Valley Collection, Lincoln Library.)

This view is on Ninth Street facing the Madison Street railroad tracks in June 1949. At right is the Central Illinois Public Service Company. At left, with the sign only partially visible, is the Barker-Lubin Company, a family-owned lumber, contracting, and home sales company. By the 1940s, the company's property holdings had expanded to include west-side property, including the site of what is now White Oaks Mall. (Courtesy of Sangamon Valley Collection, Lincoln Library.)

This *c.* 1936 street scene shows Ninth Street looking north from Jefferson Street. Many buildings in this area have long been demolished. Note the style of the traffic light at right and the white globe-topped street lights on either side. (Courtesy of Sangamon Valley Collection, Lincoln Library.)

The Great Western Railroad Depot is known for Abraham Lincoln's Farewell Address, which he delivered on February 11, 1861, at this site at Tenth and Monroe Streets. Thousands of friends and well-wishers listened to his speech and watched him depart for Washington, D.C. At that time, the depot was a one-story building. The Wabash Railroad later used it for a freight house and added the second story. (Courtesy of Sangamon Valley Collection, Lincoln Library.)

The Wolff Service Station was built in 1937 at this South Ninth Street location. By the time of this 1950s photograph, it had become Casey's Cities Service. The National Cash Register Company and Central Illinois Light Company, with its belching smokestack, can be seen behind the gas station. (Courtesy of Sangamon Valley Collection, Lincoln Library.)

This view from the middle of Ninth Street at Capitol Avenue is looking north. At left is the Sangamon County Building, completed in 1966. The modern exterior of the building was finished in granite, glass, stone, and aluminum. In the distance, also at left, is St. John's Hospital. A Route 66 sign is under the speed limit sign at right next to the utility pole. (Courtesy of Sangamon Valley Collection, Lincoln Library.)

The Sangamon County Building's dedication day was May 1, 1966. A large crowd gathered for the festivities. John B. Hendricks, chairman of the Sangamon County Board of Supervisors, served as master of ceremonies and Gov. Otto Kerner was the speaker for the dedication of the building. The Springfield Municipal Band played under the direction of Homer D. Mountz, and Viola Suits performed "The Star Spangled Banner." (Courtesy of Sangamon Valley Collection, Lincoln Library.)

The Abraham Lincoln Home at Eighth and Jackson Streets was much smaller when Abraham and Mary Todd Lincoln purchased it in 1844. They enlarged it as their family grew and lived there for 17 years. It was the only home they ever owned. The National Park Service administrates the home, which is located in the midst of a four-block area of historical homes that are undergoing restoration. (Author's collection.)

The A. Lincoln Wax Museum opened on Ninth Street close to the Abraham Lincoln Home in 1971 after a heated struggle between the city council and J. R. "Bud" Fitzpatrick, who wished to open the museum. Henry Geving was the wax sculptor and his wife, Andrea, managed the daily museum operations. A variety of tableaux featured Geving's wax sculptures of Lincoln as well as his family and associates. (Courtesy of Sangamon Valley Collection, Lincoln Library.)

This view of Ninth Street shows a mix of old and new businesses in the 1970s. The Central Illinois Ice and Cold Storage Plant was built in the early 1900s. The modern motel, car wash, and restaurant were recent additions at the time. Now the ice plant and restaurant are vacant and in disrepair. (Courtesy of Sangamon Valley Collection, Lincoln Library.)

This Standard Oil Station was at the northeast corner of Ninth and Jackson Streets. Behind it is the Central Illinois Light Company. Note the sign directing visitors to the Lincoln Depot nearby. The photograph was taken in 1971 by James A. Woodruff, who documented many sights around Springfield in the 1970s. (Courtesy of Sangamon Valley Collection, Lincoln Library.)

The Travelodge Motel and Toddle House Restaurant was located at 500 South Ninth Street, close to the Abraham Lincoln Home and other attractions. The Travelodge brand was founded by Scott King in 1939 in Southern California and advertised itself as a budget motel chain. The South Ninth Street motel was eventually demolished; a newer Travelodge is now located on South Sixth Street. (Courtesy of Sangamon Valley Collection, Lincoln Library.)

This view of the southeast corner of Ninth and Monroe Streets was taken by Mercury Studio. At center is the Central Illinois Light Company. The utility company was formed in 1913 through consolidations and purchases of other utilities. At left is the Great Western (Lincoln) Railroad Depot. (Courtesy of Sangamon Valley Collection, Lincoln Library.)

Springfield's Robert Hall Clothing Store was located on South Ninth Street. The clothing retail chain was popularly known simply as Robert Hall and was successful from around 1938 to 1966. Boomers may remember Les Paul and Mary Ford performing a commercial jingle for the chain, which began, "When the values go up, up, up; And the prices go down, down, down. Robert Hall this season; will show you the reason." (Courtesy of Sangamon Valley Collection, Lincoln Library.)

Some street repair or perhaps the unclogging of a drain is being well supervised by several onlookers in this 1950s photograph at the southwest corner of Ninth and Cass Streets. Note the familiar shield shape of the backs of the Route 66 signs. (Courtesy of Sangamon Valley Collection, Lincoln Library.)

In this photograph on Ninth Street near Spruce Street, a policeman inspects the damage done to a car when its driver ignored the barricades and drove into a hole in the street. The incident drew several onlookers. The driver of the car was taken to a local hospital. (Courtesy of Sangamon Valley Collection, Lincoln Library.)

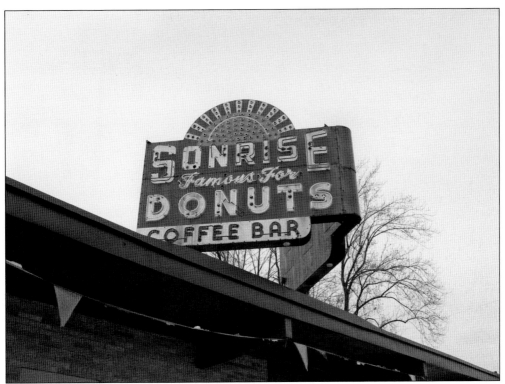

Sonrise Donuts and Coffee Bar was opened on South Grand Avenue in the 1940s by a Mr. Figura. It was said to be the first donut place in Springfield to also offer a coffee bar. Don Greenslade was an employee, and when Figura moved Sonrise Donuts to 1101 South Ninth Street, Greenslade went along, eventually buying the business. After Greenslade died, Bob Carter purchased the business and building. It now houses Gibbys Orbits, featuring donuts and a dinner menu. (Photograph by Cheryl Eichar Jett.)

This view shows construction at the intersection of Ninth Street and South Grand Avenue. A workman operated a jackhammer while another man observed. In the background, a Standard Station and lunchroom are visible. (Courtesy of Sangamon Valley Collection, Lincoln Library.)

This 1950s photograph, looking north from Laurel Street, shows major street work being done on Ninth Street. Hummer Manufacturing Company is in the background at right. The Hummer Company began in 1851 as the Post Implement Company, which manufactured plows. After buyouts, mergers, and name changes, it was purchased by Montgomery Ward and Company in 1916 and eventually renamed Hummer Manufacturing Company. (Courtesy of Sangamon Valley Collection, Lincoln Library.)

The Georgian Restaurant on the corner of Ninth Street and South Grand Avenue had a great location on Routes 66, 36, and 54. It also had plenty of parking spaces and a seating capacity of over 100. It first opened in 1941 with a seating capacity of only 18, but grew into a popular dining establishment, specializing in steaks. The restaurant closed in 1986. (Courtesy of Joe Sonderman.)

Swinney's Standard Oil Service Station was located at Eighth Street and South Grand Avenue from about 1940 through 1966. This nighttime photograph taken around 1954 shows the porcelain tile construction that was popular during that era. Porcelain facades were durable and colorfast and contributed to a sleek, modern look. That streamlined art moderne influence can be seen in

the rounded corner. Also, by this time, most gas stations were constructed with two service bays. Note the exterior clock and crown gas pump globes that further identify the style typical of the era. Proprietor E. R. Swinney featured Atlas brand tires. Three uniformed attendants were busy on the lot that night. (Courtesy of Sangamon Valley Collection, Lincoln Library.)

Tops—"Home of the Big Boy Hamburger"—became a landmark at the corner of Fifth Street and South Grand Avenue. The Big Boy restaurant chain started in California in 1936 by Bob Wian, who sold his car for $350 to open one small restaurant. It grew to be the franchising company of several hundred Big Boy locations. In Illinois, they were originally franchised simply as "Tops." (Courtesy of Sangamon Valley Collection, Lincoln Library.)

The Dew Chilli Parlor sign at this Fifth Street location near South Grand Avenue illustrates Springfield's signature spelling of the culinary creation. It is said a misspelling of the word on founder Dew Brockman's sign started it. Others say the "illi" matches the first four letters in "Illinois." In 1993, the Illinois legislature proclaimed Springfield "the Chilli Capital of the Civilized World." (Courtesy of Sangamon Valley Collection, Lincoln Library.)

This December 1950 photograph shows Rail Splitter Motor Sales (notice the Lincoln influence in the business name) at the corner of South Grand Avenue and Fifth Street. "Stop and Swap" was advertised on one of the Rail Splitter signs. The Cozy Dog House is at left. On the lamppost is a sign alerting motorists, "Traffic signal ahead Junction City 66." (Courtesy of Sue Waldmire.)

Iles Park on South Sixth Street between Oak and Ash Streets was acquired by the park district in 1903. The park consists of 10.5 acres. This delightful winter scene, taken by the Neef Studio in 1938, shows children enjoying the ice in winter. (Courtesy of Sangamon Valley Collection, Lincoln Library.)

This 1950s view looks south toward Iles Park at Oak Street. The stone park pavilion can be seen at the end of the street. The dappled shadows from many large older trees contribute to the inviting scene. The park is still a popular spot for lunch for nearby office and businesspeople, as perhaps it was for the driver of this dry cleaning truck. (Courtesy of Sangamon Valley Collection, Lincoln Library.)

The Iles Park playground was and still is a popular place for neighborhood children to play. To the north of the park is a residential area. Today there is a mix of old and new playground equipment. City sidewalks and diagonal walkways through the park provide pedestrian access for local residents. (Courtesy of Sangamon Valley Collection, Lincoln Library.)

The Top of the Arch restaurant was located on the southeast corner of South Sixth and Ash Streets on the top floor of Iles Park Place, just south of Iles Park. This restaurant and nightspot was a popular place for anniversary dinners and other special events. (Courtesy of Sangamon Valley Collection, Lincoln Library.)

This photograph shows the interior of the bar area of the Top of the Arch Restaurant at Iles Park Place at Sixth and Ash Streets in 1967. Note the piano at right and the hobnail-trimmed seating and dark ceiling beams. (Courtesy of Sangamon Valley Collection, Lincoln Library.)

Gene and Aida Petrelli were married in 1938 and owned and operated the Black Angus Steakhouse at 2242 South Sixth Street from 1953 to 1983. At one time Bo Keeley also served as host at the restaurant. Gallagher's Restaurant now occupies the building. The Black Angus chain originated in Seattle; today there are 46 steak houses located only in western states. (Author's collection.)

The Bel-Aire Manor Motel at 2636 South Sixth Street advertised itself in 1954 as "one of Springfield's newest and finest motels." Located on the south side of the city on Business Route 66, it was in an "area of modern restaurants and supper clubs." One of their postcards advised, "Be sure to visit the Lincoln shrines, Lake Springfield, and the state buildings." (Courtesy of Joe Sonderman.)

Eighty modern units at the Bel-Aire Manor Motel made it one of the larger motels in the area. The units were equipped with electric and hot water heat, carpeting, tile baths, television, telephones, hotel furniture, music by Muzak, and "other modern appointments." The Bel-Aire was built in 1951. (Courtesy of Joe Sonderman.)

A later view of the Bel-Aire Manor Motel showed the second-story addition all the way around with an attractive fountain and landscaping in front. The original design of the Bel-Aire was an L-shaped building with gable-end roofs and two-story columned sections. (Courtesy of Joe Sonderman.)

The Supper Club was located at 2641 South Sixth Street. Here its interior looks ready for business. The club's advertisements billed it as "Springfield's finest supper club and cocktail lounge . . . featuring steak, chicken, and sea foods." Vito Impastato was the manager at the time this photograph was taken. (Courtesy of Sangamon Valley Collection, Lincoln Library.)

The interior of the Plantation Restaurant at 2705 South Sixth Street looks welcoming with its checked tablecloths and neat rows of tables and chairs. The smiling bartender and well-stocked bar appear to be ready to welcome customers in this c. 1956 photograph. (Courtesy of Sangamon Valley Collection, Lincoln Library.)

HUNGRY? DRIVE OVER TO McDONALD'S

HAMBURGERS	15 CENTS
CHEESEBURGERS	19 CENTS
TRIPLE THICK SHAKES	20 CENTS
FRENCH FRIES	10 CENTS
COKE	10 CENTS
MILK–COFFEE	10 CENTS
ORANGEADE	10 CENTS
ROOT BEER	10 CENTS

2849 So. 6TH St.

JUST OPPOSITE ALLIS CHALMERS MAIN GATE   SPRINGFIELD, ILLINOIS

An advertisement for McDonald's offers hamburgers for 15¢ and cheeseburgers for 19¢ at its 2849 South Sixth Street location "just opposite Allis Chalmers Main Gate." This location opened around 1955. John Mack Sr. owned McDonald's restaurants in Springfield until his death in 1974 at age 61. (Courtesy of Sangamon Valley Collection, Lincoln Library.)

At 2901 South Sixth Street, the Sinclair Service Station and Sixth Street Grill offered travelers food, lodging, and automobile service. This light-colored brick building was constructed with a flat roof and dentil molding. Note the exterior clock that was popular at the time, the Coca-Cola sign over the grill window, and the woody wagon with its hood up. (Courtesy of Sangamon Valley Collection, Lincoln Library.)

A. LINCOLN TOURIST COURT — U. S. 66 — SOUTH LIMITS OF
SPRINGFIELD, ILLINOIS

The A. Lincoln Tourist Court was built at 2927 South Sixth Street in the late 1940s. This view shows the motel units, office, and home of Mr. and Mrs. W. D. Posegate, the owners/managers. The "ultra modern" brick construction court contained 24 units, each with a tile bath and "year-round comfort." (Courtesy of Joe Sonderman.)

In this view from the east side of Sixth Street, the individual garages for the A. Lincoln Tourist Court units can be seen. Five more tile bath units had been added by the time this postcard was printed. The tourist court was American Automobile Association (AAA) recommended. (Courtesy of Joe Sonderman.)

In a later photograph, the name has been changed to A. Lincoln Motel, and an attractive fence and a larger sign with Lincoln's image has been added. There were now 38 motel units with room telephones, air-conditioners, and television. (Courtesy of Joe Sonderman.)

The A. Lincoln Motel had added a swimming pool and four more motel units by the printing of this postcard. Despite all the improvements, the motel was eventually torn down. When the 1950 Cozy Dog Drive In building was demolished to make way for a new Walgreens store, a new Cozy Dog Drive In building was built on the site of the A. Lincoln Motel. (Courtesy of Joe Sonderman.)

Ed Waldmire Jr. hands a "Cozy Dog" to his wife, Ginny, at the Lake Springfield Beach House in 1946 as they launch their Cozy Dog venture. Waldmire had been intrigued by a sandwich called a "corn dog" out in Oklahoma, but it took too long to prepare. Later Waldmire heard from his friend Don Strand who had developed a batter mix that would stick on a wiener while it was French-fried. (Courtesy of Sue Waldmire.)

After the successful launch at the Lake Springfield Beach House, the next step was a booth at the Illinois State Fair that same summer. Here is the Cozy Dog booth featuring the "G.I. Hot Dog" at the fair in August 1946. (Courtesy of Sue Waldmire.)

The Waldmires's first permanent Cozy Dog House was on South Grand Avenue between Fifth and Sixth Streets next to Rail Splitters Auto Sales. Undoubtedly, by this time, Ed Waldmire was glad that his wife, Ginny, had suggested that he drop his original name for the improved corn dog—the "Crusty Cur"—and call it a "Cozy Dog." (Courtesy of Sue Waldmire.)

The interior of the new Cozy Dog Drive In on South Sixth Street is shown here on grand-opening day, September 27, 1950. Notice the snappy white uniform on the young waiter at far left. Plants and flowers from well-wishers lined the wall under the windows of the dining room. (Courtesy of Sue Waldmire.)

On Mother's Day in 1952, from left to right, Ann Williams, Leona Beckes, and MariJane Waldmire were working as Cozy Dog waitresses and wearing flower corsages. Cozy Dog has always been known for retaining employees for a long period of time. Now Ed Waldmire's daughter-in-law Sue Waldmire, along with her sons, operates the Cozy Dog. (Courtesy of Sue Waldmire.)

This is a counter model deep fat fryer designed specifically for corn dogs. One person could dip three wieners in batter while, at the same time, cooking three Cozy Dogs using the specially designed holders. An extra corn dog holder rests in a rack attached to the fryer. This production-line approach combined with Don Strand's improved batter mix was faster and more efficient than dipping and frying Cozy Dogs individually. (Courtesy of Sue Waldmire.)

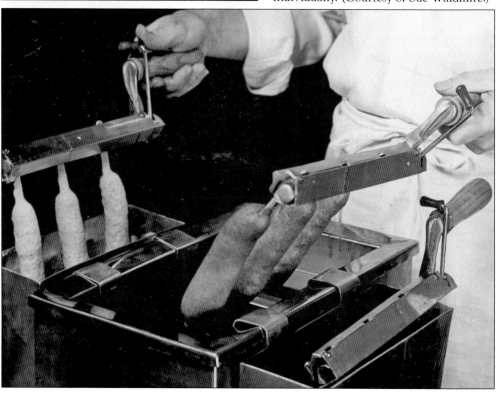

Ed Waldmire (right) and his manager are pictured here in front of the new Cozy Dog and Dairy Queen building on South Sixth Street ready for customers to arrive on grand-opening day in September 1950. Cozy Dog operated in this building until 1996, when it moved into its current location at 2935 South Sixth Street right next door to the north of this building. Walgreens now occupies this spot. (Courtesy of Sue Waldmire.)

In this 1953 photograph of the Allis-Chalmers plant, the large smokestack dominates the view. The Monarch Tractor Company relocated to Springfield in 1924 from Watertown, Wisconsin, after a brief move to Chicago. In 1928, the Monarch Tractor Company was bought by Allis-Chalmers. (Courtesy of Sangamon Valley Collection, Lincoln Library.)

The sprawling Allis-Chalmers plant, looking from the northwest toward Lake Springfield, is seen in this c. 1970 view. In the 1970s, its construction division was sold to Fiat, and the Springfield plant became known as Fiat-Allis. For many years, the name Allis-Chalmers was synonymous with its trademark orange tractors. (Courtesy of Sangamon Valley Collection, Lincoln Library.)

In another aerial view, taken earlier than the one above, Allis-Chalmers can be seen, identified by its factory sprawl and tall smokestack. In the back toward the left is the Illinois State Capitol and to its right is downtown Springfield. In the foreground, situated at an angle, is St. Joseph's Home. At left along the street is Copp's Corner, consisting of six buildings built by Melio Copp. (Courtesy of Sangamon Valley Collection, Lincoln Library.)

This row of buildings in the 3200 block of South Sixth Street Road was built by Melio Copp in the 1920s. A sign on the third building proclaims, "Welcome to Copp's Corner." A gas station, grocery store, icehouse, barbershop, cabins, and auto garage (later turned into a locker plant for Pegwill Packing Company) provided just about everything that a motorist might need, all on one corner. (Courtesy of Sangamon Valley Collection, Lincoln Library.)

According to his daughter Mary Catherine Copp, Frank Marion Joseph "Melio" Copp built all six commercial buildings in the 3200 block of South Sixth Street Road. Mary Catherine wrote notes about her family and the businesses at Copp's Corner on the backs of this series of photographs before donating them to the Sangamon Valley Collection. (Courtesy of Sangamon Valley Collection, Lincoln Library.)

The house near the center of the photograph was moved to the Copp's Corner site from elsewhere. The grocery store was built next to it and housed a grocery business and a barbershop downstairs and apartments upstairs. A note on the back of this photograph stated that the cabins were the "first ones around" and that "we never lived in the house." A United Community Bank, McDonald's, and Arby's surround the one surviving original building, which is now the home of the Curve Inn. (Courtesy of Sangamon Valley Collection, Lincoln Library.)

The small building at left was the icehouse, and the building at right was White's Auto Garage. The dark-colored building at center was the Shell Service Station, also selling Goodyear tires. Notice the visible-gas pumps in the shadow of the roof overhang. Melio Copp, his wife Mary Ann, and their baby Mary Catherine lived in the back of the Shell Service Station building. (Courtesy of Sangamon Valley Collection, Lincoln Library.)

This photograph was taken at the Shell Service Station at Copp's Corner. Melio Copp is at right, pumping gas. The mother and son at left are Pauline Copp Pleshe and Robert Pleshe, sister and nephew to Melio Copp. The visible-gas pumps and the oil containers identify this as an early gas station. (Courtesy of Sangamon Valley Collection, Lincoln Library.)

The interior of the Shell Service Station offered a variety of goods for sale—displayed on shelves and in glass cases. Notice the bare lightbulbs at the back and the tobacco, cigarette, and seed posters. Behind the counter is Pauline Copp Pleshe. (Courtesy of Sangamon Valley Collection, Lincoln Library.)

In front of the Shell Service Station at Copp's Corner are, from left to right, the Shell Oil Company representative (name unknown) with sister and brother Pauline Copp Pleshe and Melio Copp. Later, in the 1940s, a section of one of the buildings was made into an apartment for Bill Wingerter, well known in Springfield as "Pegwill Pete," owner of the Pegwill Packing Company. (Courtesy of Sangamon Valley Collection, Lincoln Library.)

The Comerford Inn was one of the new buildings constructed on Copp's Corner. The Comerford family operated the tavern from about 1932 until 1945. From left to right are Maryln Smith, Marie Comerford Smith Joyce, Frances Comerford, Mattie Comerford, Martha Comerford, and Lawrence Comerford. (Courtesy of Sangamon Valley Collection, Lincoln Library.)

The Comerford Inn was purchased in 1945 by Guido Manci, who renamed it the Curve Inn, after the curve in Route 66 around Copp's Corner. The Curve Inn developed a scandalous reputation for illegal gambling and a buzzer at the back stairs for admittance to the "ladies' apartments" upstairs. In 1972, Neil McGillivray purchased the bar and kept the Curve Inn name. It is now owned by Ray and Ami Merchant and Don Thompson. (Photograph by Cheryl Eichar Jett.)

This 1939 photograph shows, from left to right, daughter Mary Catherine Copp (no longer a baby as she was when the family moved to the corner), Marion Joseph "Melio" Copp, and his wife, Mary Ann. They posed for this photograph while visiting the World's Fair in New York City. (Courtesy of Sangamon Valley Collection, Lincoln Library.)

The Kerasotes Route 66 Drive-In Theatre opened just off Route 66 on St. Joseph's Road in the summer of 1952. The new drive-in featured "a screen tower 80 feet wide by 80 feet high (approximate height of a seven-story building)," according to the *Illinois State Journal*. There were 1,307 speakers and the latest in electronic and projection equipment. Opening movies were *Double Crossbones* with Donald O'Connor and *Cattle Drive* with Joel McCrea. (Courtesy of Sangamon Valley Collection, Lincoln Library.)

St. Joseph's Home at 3306 South Sixth Street Road was completed in 1925. The Sisters of St. Francis of the Immaculate Conception established its mission of caring for the aged and infirm persons with love and respect over 100 years ago, and they continue to manage the home today. The home began in the Wabash Railroad Hospital, formerly the home of James Cook Conkling, at Sixth and Lawrence Streets in 1903. (Photograph by Cheryl Eichar Jett.)

The Southern View Motel and Dining Room at 720 St. Joseph Street offered in-room phones, air-conditioning, television, Simmons Beautyrest mattresses, wall-to-wall carpeting, ceramic tile baths, and if needed, baby cribs. The motel also featured a conference room, dining room, and deck with umbrella tables. (Courtesy of Joe Sonderman.)

Gene and Carman Schultz were the managers of the Southern View Motel. Although the motel's address was St. Joseph Street (from St. Joseph's Home nearby), it was adjacent to Route 66 and very accessible to travelers. (Courtesy of Joe Sonderman.)

The Southern View Motel's big, modern sign brought travelers in off Route 66, and the motel had plenty of units and parking spaces to accommodate them. At left, the tall smokestack identifies Allis-Chalmers to the north. (Courtesy of Joe Sonderman.)

The Ramada Inn at 3751 South Sixth Street was a later addition to Springfield's lineup of motels. The Ramada offered complete hotel service with 125 "beautifully-decorated" rooms. The motel boasted meeting rooms, a cocktail lounge, a dining room and coffee shop, a heated swimming pool, and year-round air-conditioning. (Author's collection.)

An early view of the Lamp Liter Tourist Lodge south of Springfield shows just a few units in a decidedly rural setting. A fenced area has hammocks and lawn chairs for relaxation. (Courtesy of Sangamon Valley Collection, Lincoln Library.)

As shown in this view, the Lamp Liter Lodge has clearly expanded on its 8-acre site. It was associated with the Best Western Motels and American Automobile Association (AAA) and boasted a fireplace and a color television in the lobby. At the time of this postcard, James R. Grady was the owner/general manager, and Virgil Dial Jr. was the dining room manager. (Courtesy of Sangamon Valley Collection, Lincoln Library.)

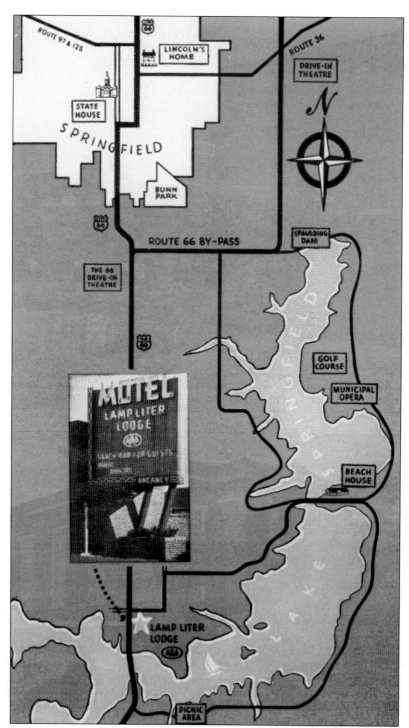

This postcard features a handy map of Springfield, main routes and attractions, Lake Springfield, and of course, the Lamp Liter Lodge. Route 66 is clearly pictured cutting north to south through Springfield, and Bypass 66 is shown southeast of the heart of Springfield. (Courtesy of Joe Sonderman.)

The Lake View Cabins were located 6 miles south of Springfield on the lake, "air-conditioned by the lake breeze." Lake View advertisements invited guests to "enjoy our home cooking, home made chili, milk shakes, and ice cream." Guests could fish, eat, or stay cozy in the "rock wall insulated cabins." Adolph Bedini was the proprietor. (Courtesy of Joe Sonderman.)

The Colonial Tourist Home was a two-story home converted into tourist quarters 6 miles south of Springfield on Route 66 near Lake Springfield. It was advertised to be "cool and pleasant" with both hot and cold water in the rooms. Rates were $2 and up for couples. Mr. and Mrs. H. J. Hoechster were the proprietors. (Courtesy of Joe Sonderman.)

SOUTH SIXTH STREET BRIDGE ON U. S. ROUTE 66, SPRINGFIELD, ILL.

The beautiful old bridge with its tall lights, located on Route 66 over Lake Springfield, was created in the 1930s and constructed to carry traffic over the lake. The lake itself is a man-made 4,200-acre reservoir and is the largest municipally owned lake in Illinois. (Courtesy of Joe Sonderman.)

In a 1950s aerial view, looking north, Route 66 is clearly seen across Lake Springfield. In the foreground is the state police station. The route cuts through a patchwork of farmland on its way to the city. (Courtesy of Sangamon Valley Collection, Lincoln Library.)

Four

THE 1940–1977 ALIGNMENT

Bypass 66 was designated to move traffic, once again, farther from the center of the city. This alignment moved Route 66 farther to the east, diverting it from Peoria Road near the Illinois State Fairgrounds onto Thirty-first Street, later renamed Dirksen Parkway for U.S. Senator Everett McKinley Dirksen. Restaurants, truck stops, motels, service stations, and automobile dealers flourished on this route, serving the vacationers and the truckers. Bergen Park Golf Course was along the route, as was the Springfield Drive-In Theatre and the Springfield Speedway. The newly created Illinois Department of Transportation moved into their new home, the modern-looking Harry R. Hanley Building. At the south end of Dirksen Parkway, traffic turned right onto Adlai Stevenson Drive, formerly Linn Avenue. Eventually traffic could also turn to the left onto the new interstate, I-55. Along Stevenson Drive, going east, more motels and restaurants appeared, along with a mixture of retail businesses and state headquarters, such as the Illinois Baptist Association's new building and the Veterans of Foreign Wars' new state offices. At the east end of Stevenson Drive, Bypass 66 rejoined City 66 and moved south on South Sixth Street.

Videe Pottery and China Company was located on Bypass 66 north of Springfield. The store advertised that it was one of the largest stores of its kind. Videe sold unusual glass, china, pottery, gifts, collectors' items, and imports. (Courtesy of Joe Sonderman.)

ROSEWOOD STEAK HOUSE, BY-PASS 66 N., SPRINGFIELD, ILL.

The Rosewood Steakhouse was located a block north of North Grand Avenue on Bypass 66. On their menu they offered steaks and "tempting Athenian fried chicken." The attractive dining room was furnished with white tablecloths and a polished hardwood floor. Food was served "in an atmosphere of refinement and friendliness." (Courtesy of Joe Sonderman.)

The Shamrock Court Motel was located north on Bypass 66, across the street from the popular Fleetwood Restaurant. The motel featured telephones, television, carpet, and air-conditioning. The small motel was constructed in 1953 in a rectangular shape with about eight units and was formerly known as the Akers Motel. It is still standing today and in business, advertising weekly rates. (Courtesy of Joe Sonderman.)

The Caravan Motel was built in 1953 and was later known as the Dirksen Inn. On Bypass 66 North, it featured eight units with tile baths, air-conditioning, automatic heat, and Simmons Beautyrest mattresses and claimed to be fireproof. Mr. and Mrs. Ira E. Tosh were the owners/managers of the "place with the friendly air." The building is still there, just south of the Shamrock Court, but the sign is gone. (Courtesy of Joe Sonderman.)

The Fleetwood Restaurant at 855 North Thirty-First Street became a landmark on Bypass 66 for hungry travelers. The doors were opened in early 1957 by Tony and Opal Lauck with assistance from their children, Linda and Dan, plus 15 employees. Lauck was a 20-year veteran of restaurant management before opening the Fleetwood as a 135-seat truck stop. Two years later, the popular menu item known as broasted chicken was added to their menu. (Courtesy of Joe Sonderman.)

FLEETWOOD RESTAURANT – U. S. 66 & 54 BY-PASS SPRINGFIELD, ILL.

In 1979, Linda Lauck and her husband, John Howard, became the owners/operators of the Fleetwood. By this time, highway traffic had been going by Springfield on I-55 for a decade and a half. The Laucks concentrated their efforts on transforming the Fleetwood into a local family restaurant, and in the 1980s, remodeling and additions produced a garden room, a drive-up window, and a remodeled coffee shop. (Courtesy of Joe Sonderman.)

This image of the Fleetwood Restaurant at night highlights the large sign that hailed travelers and locals for 36 years. In the late 1970s, the restaurant was serving over 3,000 people every weekend. But the abundance of franchise restaurants and labor shortages were cited as reasons for closing the Fleetwood's doors in 1993. The signposts are still there. (Courtesy of Joe Sonderman.)

BROADVIEW MOTOR COURT
U.S. 54, Junction By Pass 66
SPRINGFIELD, ILLINOIS

The Broadview Motor Court was located at 3116 Sangamon Avenue, not far from the Illinois State Fairgrounds and close to Bypass 66. Owner Witt Workman was an early member of Best Western Motels. (Courtesy of Joe Sonderman.)

H-V MOTEL - BY PASS 66 - ½ MILE NORTH 36 - SPRINGFIELD, ILLINOIS

The H-V Motel was located on a tree-shaded spot on Bypass 66 near Route 36. The motel, located at 444 North Thirty-first Street (later known as Dirksen Parkway), featured eight units in an L-shaped brick building with a gable roof. The motel is no longer there. (Courtesy of Joe Sonderman.)

On Christmas Day in 1942, an A-20 Boston Bomber landed safely on Bypass 66 when it was about to run out of fuel. The pilot's skill was praised, as he managed to land the plane with "only 9 inches clearance between the telephone poles," according to the *Illinois State Journal*. After obtaining fuel and enjoying neighbors' hospitality, the pilot, Lt. John Graybill, took off from Bypass 66. (Courtesy of Bill Shea Sr.)

The Parkview Motel at 3121 Clear Lake Avenue was built in 1950 near Bergen Park "overlooking the city golf course" and operated by the Jerry Burke family. It featured 22 units with room phones, televisions, electric heat, and air-conditioning. A free snack bar and coffee in the rooms were additional enticements. (Courtesy of Joe Sonderman.)

The Fireside Restaurant at Route 29 and Bypass 66 was located in a one-story building shared with Joy Transfer Company. Jasper Thompson and his son were the proprietors. An extensive menu included chicken, steaks, fish, and Italian dishes. The Fireside's postcard advertised a seating capacity of 200 and a reminder that there was "no liquor served." (Courtesy of Joe Sonderman.)

Enjoying the Day at Bergen Park.

In 1912, Catherine Bergen Jones, at age 96, asked the City of Springfield to call this tract of land purchased for "pleasure grounds" Bergen Park after her father, the Rev. John D. Bergen. The Bergen Park tract had been the Bergen farm and Catherine Bergen Jones's home. According to the *Illinois State Journal*, Reverend Bergen had taught at Princeton and settled in Illinois in 1828. The first Presbyterian minister in Springfield, he began the first temperance society in central Illinois and contributed funds to many community projects. Bergen began writing for various newspapers in the state and used as his pen name "the old man of the prairie." Bergen Park has been a popular golf course since the early 1900s. (Courtesy of Sangamon Valley Collection, Lincoln Library.)

The Springfield Drive-In Theater was built and opened in 1947 at the corner of Bypass 66 and Route 29. It could accommodate 800 cars in its 60,000-square-yard area. Patrons without cars could find comfortable chairs waiting for them. A newspaper story explained that "another convenience that this type of theater boasts is the eliminating of the need for dressing up in order to enjoy a movie." (Courtesy of Sangamon Valley Collection, Lincoln Library.)

A 1950s aerial photograph of the Springfield Drive-In shows the size of the movie screen structure compared to the size of buildings down the road. It was said to be the world's largest movie screen at 62 feet by 46 feet. The screen tower itself rose 76 feet from the ground. A refreshment stand, which was added in 1953, suffered $20,000 in damages in a 1968 fire. The theater closed around 1984. (Courtesy of Sangamon Valley Collection, Lincoln Library.)

Joe Shaheen's Springfield Speedway was popular with automobile racing enthusiasts throughout the Midwest. Shaheen, a successful businessman and Midget Racer fan, constructed a quarter-mile track in the late 1940s. It came to be known as "Little Springfield" in contrast to the mile-long track at the Illinois State Fairgrounds. Midget racing gave way to stock cars and modifieds; well-known names from many states raced here up to its close in 1988. (Courtesy of Sangamon Valley Collection, Lincoln Library.)

The 77th Illinois General Assembly formed the Illinois Department of Transportation (IDOT) in 1972. IDOT is housed in the Harry R. Hanley Building at 2300 South Dirksen Parkway. The department's predecessor was the Illinois Department of Public Works and Buildings. The Public Works and Buildings Department was authorized in 1921 to hire Illinois State Highway Patrol officers. By 1922, eight officers earning $150 per month each were patrolling the entire state. (Photograph by Cheryl Eichar Jett.)

Along the various alignments of Route 66, automobile-related businesses soon developed. In the 3000 block of South Thirty-first Street/South Dirksen Parkway, this 1977 photograph exhibits a variety of such offerings. A used-car lot and a truck stop are at left with a Site Service Station at right. Notice the upside-down "Father's Day special" at the car lot and the 58¢ per gallon gas price at the Site Service Station. (Courtesy of Sangamon Valley Collection, Lincoln Library.)

116

The Holiday Inn East was built in 1964 at the intersection of Bypass 66 and I-55; its street address was 3100 South Dirksen Parkway. The modern motel boasted both an indoor and an outdoor pool and two coffee shops. Plenty of parking and 401 units accommodated travelers. This Holiday Inn postcard also highlighted the hotel's large banquet space for up to 1,501 persons. (Author's collection.)

The smokestacks of City Water, Light, and Power's plants have been a landmark at the southeast corner of the city since the mid-1930s. At that time, the utility constructed its original facility, the Lakeside Power Station, on the shore of the then-new Lake Springfield. Lakeside consisted of eight boilers, decreasing to seven by the 1960s. After the construction of the new power station in 2009, the last two remaining Lakeside units became non-operational. (Photograph by Cheryl Eichar Jett.)

Denny's Restaurant, located on Stevenson Drive close to the intersection with Dirksen Parkway and access to the new I-55, is shown here in April 1977. This is the same year that Denny's introduced the Grand Slam breakfast as a nod to Hank Aaron. The chain numbered over 1,000 Denny's restaurants by 1981. (Courtesy of Sangamon Valley Collection, Lincoln Library.)

Biederman Furniture Company was located at 2713 Stevenson Drive. It was housed in a new one-story, buff-brick building, which covered nearly an acre, accompanied by a spacious parking lot and landscaped grounds. This was the 13th store for the St. Louis–based company. An early sales crew included Jerry Davincen, John Abel, Dick Pitchford, Thomas Jett, and Paul Malady, who was known for performing a run through the store ending with a jump to demonstrate mattress quality. (Courtesy of Sangamon Valley Collection, Lincoln Library.)

The Hazel Dell Sinclair Service Station at 2604 Stevenson Drive was one of the early service stations along Linn Avenue, as it was known in 1951 when this photograph was taken. Linn Avenue was renamed Adlai Stevenson Drive in 1966 in honor of the 1949–1953 Illinois governor and 1961–1965 U.S. Ambassador to the United Nations. Notice the Linn Avenue Chili Parlor to the left. (Courtesy of Sangamon Valley Collection, Lincoln Library.)

The Illini Motor Company built a new modern building at 1829 Stevenson Drive in 1966. The *Springfield Sun* hailed the new facilities as "outstanding and different in appearance from any other automobile showroom and offices in this area." The smaller section at left housed the offices, and the larger section was the showroom. A repair shop and service area were located in the rear. This was proof "that Springfield is on the move," according to the newspaper article. (Courtesy of Sangamon Valley Collection, Lincoln Library.)

The Evening Star Motel at 1409 Linn Avenue was one of the early motels in this area of Springfield. It offered tiled shower baths, individual thermostat-controlled steam heat, air-conditioning, television, in-room phones, baby cribs, and a restaurant nearby. The early-format phone number was 4-4737. (Courtesy of Joe Sonderman.)

This 1966 photograph shows the construction of the new Howard Johnson Motor Lodge and Restaurant on Stevenson Drive adjacent to I-55 and Route 66. The company reached its peak in 1975, but just a few years later, the end of the company appeared inevitable. Revenue from travelers had fallen off in the 1970s due to the 1974 oil embargo, and their traditional dining-room fare was costly in comparison to the new fast food chains, which appealed to families. (Courtesy of Sangamon Valley Collection, Lincoln Library.)

Five

HISTORIC ROUTE 66 TODAY

Today the instantly recognizable brown Historic Route 66 signs guide visitors along the various alignments through Springfield. Travelers and Route 66 fans enjoy driving these routes, viewing the original sites that are still there, and imagining those that are gone. Route 66 organizations, historians, preservationists, and aficionados have worked alongside the National Park Service and the Illinois Department of Transportation to keep the memory of Route 66 alive. Too many individuals to name have contributed in many ways. Some of the old businesses are still in operation, while new ones have established themselves. Some sites and highway segments are on the National Register of Historic Places, and much documentation has been done. Many baby boomers remember childhood family vacations on the famous highway and want to relive those memories. For all these reasons, Route 66 still lives.

Bob Waldmire, one of Ed and Ginny Waldmire's sons, was an artist and illustrator of Route 66. He grew up watching the cars go by on Route 66; a family road trip to California in 1962 was the confirmation of his desire to simply travel Route 66. A talented illustrator, he supported his Route 66 travel with his artwork. He was truly a free spirit, living in his converted school bus in Rochester, Illinois, and traveling in his Volkswagen bus. He also lived in Hackberry, Arizona, at his Old Route 66 Visitor Center and Preservation Foundation. The *Chicago Tribune*, the *State Journal-Register*, *Illinois Times*, and various Route 66 publications all wrote about him. The *Wall Street Journal* called him "King of Route 66." In December 2009, Bob Waldmire lost his battle with cancer. (Both courtesy of Sue Waldmire.)

In Williamsville, just a few miles north of Springfield on old Route 66, Die Cast Auto Sales is housed in a converted 1930s service station. On display is a collection of Route 66 souvenirs, Coca-Cola collectibles, and die-cast models. Originally a railroad village, the community was called Benton and later renamed Williamsville in honor of Col. John Williams, a local landowner. Several historic buildings remain, and the Williamsville Historical Museum occupies two railroad boxcars. Pictured are Frank and Jackie Kohlrus, owners of Die Cast Auto Sales. (Courtesy of Springfield Convention and Visitors Bureau.)

One of the original screens from the Green Meadows Drive-In is pictured here at the Route 66 Twin Drive-In on Recreation Drive south of Springfield between I-55 and Illinois Route 4. The Green Meadows Drive-In Theatre was opened in Green Meadows Recreation Park in 1973 by Mid-America Theatres. The Knight family purchased the property in 1992 and reopened the drive-in theater in 2002, with both screens refurbished, the concession building completely remodeled, and the sound transmitted over an FM station for each screen. (Courtesy of Knight's Action Park.)

One block south of the Illinois State Fairgrounds on Peoria Road, Shea's Gas Station Museum is a not-to-be-missed attraction. Bill Shea Sr. opened his Texaco Station down the street in the 1940s. In 1955, he moved to his present location and opened a Marathon Station. Along the way he continued collecting gas pumps, signs, Route 66 memorabilia, and stories. Today the father-and-son team of Bill Shea Sr. and Bill Shea Jr. welcome visitors for a $2 admission fee. (Courtesy of Springfield Convention and Visitors Bureau.)

Mel-O-Cream Donuts was established as a retail shop in Springfield in 1932 by Kelly Grant Sr. Since this was the time of the Great Depression, Grant made ends meet by selling donuts at wholesale to restaurants and grocery stores. Word spread, and the Mel-O-Cream business grew. In 1954, it became incorporated, and his son Kelly Grant Jr. acquired the company. There are several Mel-O-Cream locations today in Springfield. (Photograph by Cheryl Eichar Jett.)

Joe Rogers opened the Den Chili Parlor at 1125 South Grand Avenue on December 31, 1945. Although the small restaurant only had 11 stools at the counter and no tables, customers flocked to the restaurant. Joe and Pauline Rogers's daughter Marianne continued the family tradition with a Den Chili Parlor location at 820 South Ninth Street/City 66, pictured here. All her parents' recipes are still followed. The Den is still open, but Marianne has recently retired. (Photograph by Cheryl Eichar Jett.)

Historic Route 66 signs denoting the various alignments (1926–1930, 1930–1940, 1940–1977) through Springfield are plentiful throughout the Springfield area. Besides being helpful reminders to the Historic Route 66 traveler that one is indeed on the right street or road, they are also a nod to a special part of Springfield's history. The brown Historic Route 66 signs were installed in the 1990s by the Illinois Department of Transportation. (Photograph by Cheryl Eichar Jett.)

Each September, the International Route 66 Mother Road Festival attracts tens of thousands of Route 66 fans to downtown Springfield. The rumble of engines from classic vehicles mixes with live music from outdoor stages. Vendors, souvenirs, Route 66 celebrities, food, and kids' activities round out the event. Route 66 is not forgotten. (Courtesy of Springfield Convention and Visitors Bureau.)

BIBLIOGRAPHY

Barton-Aschman Associates, Inc., in association with Archaeological Research, Inc. *Route 66 Operational Guidelines*. Prepared for the Illinois Department of Transportation, revised May 1997.

Dimont, Kathy, et al. *Special Resource Study: Route 66*. National Park Service, July 1995.

Illinois State Journal

Kirchner, Charles, Charles Kirchner and Associates, Ltd. *Lazy A. Motel*. National Register of Historic Places Registration Form, 1994.

Power, J. C. *History of Springfield Illinois*. Reprinted by BiblioLife, LLC, 2009.

Seratt, Dorothy R. L. and Ryburn-Lamont, Terri, Route 66 Association of Illinois. *Historic and Architectural Resources of Route 66 Through Illinois*. National Register of Historic Places Multiple Property Documentation Form, 1997.

Springfield City Directories

Springfield Sun

State Journal-Register

Teague, Tom, Friends of the Sangamon Valley. *Route 66 by Carpenter Park*. National Register of Historic Places Registration Form, 2002.

Weiss, John. *Traveling the . . . New, Historic Route 66 of Illinois*. Wilmington, IL: John Weiss, 1997.

www.byways.org (National Scenic Byways Program)

www.digitalroute66.com (Digital Route 66)

www.illinoisroute66.org (Illinois Route 66 Scenic Byway)

www.nps.gov (National Park Service)

www.arcadiapublishing.com

Discover books about the town where you grew up, the cities where your friends and families live, the town where your parents met, or even that retirement spot you've been dreaming about. Our Web site provides history lovers with exclusive deals, advanced notification about new titles, e-mail alerts of author events, and much more.

Find Your Place in History.